Daily dose of Dee's feelings

DALYA AHMED

Presentation by *BookLeaf Publishing*

Web: www.bookleafpub.com

E-mail: info@bookleafpub.com

ISBN: 978-93-95890-47-2

First edition 2022

How to love

Handle with care
Is what her eyes read
Love my feats and flaws
Are the words she never said
Give me security and I'll give you the world
Those weren't the only words he heard
He heard her screams for serenity
He promised her love for eternity
She didn't mean to be too much
She didn't feel the two souls touch
They instantly became one
And she just wanted to teach him how to love

I love you

I wish to rest my tired bones
In the warmth of your embrace
Lay my body next to yours
Finally face to face
I've been searching for someone like you
For far too long
The connection we have, the obstacles we have
overcome
Made this so strong
With your skin oh so smooth on mine
Our hearts and bodies intertwined
Could this be? Just you and me?
Uniting as one
Forever and always, plus one
Because this isn't just any connection
I'm not just looking for some attention
I love you, with all I am
With every fiber in my being
And every ounce in me
I love you, for all of you
For your heart and soul
For you being with me

I heard

I heard youre not too well
I'm not doing any better
I feel like we are living in hell
I'll just write you a letter
I'll tell you I hope youre doing okay
I'll tell you things will get better one day
I'll try to write all the things Ive beern menaing
to say
I apologize if my tears stain the letter
I apologize my tears keep getting wetter
Its almost time to make a wish and im torn
between two
I wish that you either get through or that I never
met you
Is this love in my head?
have we ever taken a step ahead?
if i could just take you in my arms once more
hide you from your pain and your internal war
id kiss your forehead so you feel relieved
id make you feel less deceived
just know i will always remember
and be here for you
yes theres emptiness inside me
and a hole in my chest too

i'll scribble x's and o's along with my name on
the bottom
just in case you never want to see it
i'll be sure to put out the spark you seem to have
accidentally lit.

I will destroy you

I will destroy you
And I won't even be around
You'll touch her but you will feel me
You will see her but you'll see my eyes
When you take a breath my scent will float
around you
You took such a big part of me when you left me
But I'll always be with you in heart but not for
you
And you'll see pictures of me here and there
And I hope to God that when you do
You feel the same passionate hell I did when I
was without you
And you never ever get the feel of security as
you have to give to get and you never gave me
that sense not one bit

It's true I crave you

I crave you in the most innocent form.
I crave to say good night and give you forehead
kisses and to say I adore you when you feel at
your worst. I crave you in ways where I just
want to be next to you and nothing more or less.

May raining

I always feel the want to need you
And I always need to want you
But I don't know which ones worse
I'll almost always miss you
And I never want to be without you
But I don't know if its a blessing or a curse
Because I feel everything and anything with you
And I can't see anyone for me but you
But I don't know how I make you feel
So let me know
If I make you feel as alive as you do to me
Let me back in your heart, and forever yours I'll
be.
I remember running my fingers through your
hair
I remember inhaling your cologne and my eyes
rolling back
I see you all around me and long to feel you
everywhere

In the heat

He stares her down
She does the same
Why would you say that
She glares
Who told you that
He questions
They fuss and fight all through the night
And sleep on opposite sides of the bed
Noone is going to admit the other is right
The lights are dim and the streetlight is
flickering and then it's dead
In the heat of it all, their bodies come closer
They forget what started this all, and
remembered their promises to eachother to
always be closer
Their bodies become one
Their souls reunite
In the heat

Carelessness

Why don't you notice me
She thinks it's her in hesitation
I dyed my hair and cut it
He looks at her in admiration
She sits across from him with a book in her
hands
He holds his phone up as if to get a few bars
If I twirl my hair will you notice me
Her heart races imagining it
If I get a new piercing will you care
He holds his hand out imagining where her
fingers would perfectly fit
He looks at her through a camera lens in
adoration
She looks the other way, foolishly thinking he's
full of carelessness

Jealousy

They say sadness kills
And heartbreak too
But you know what noone admits?
Jealousy does too
She wouldn't choose you if she didn't want you
He wouldn't ask you so much if he did trust you
She chose you and continue ls to do so
But you still listen to your demons, they bring
you to the lowest of low
Your love is all I need til the end
She tells him
But your jealousy is going to bring this all to end

Happiness

Happiness is all I feel with you
Like a little kid in a candy store
Happiness is all you give me
Like a winning buzzer with the final score
Happiness is all I feel with you
And all I want in the world is you
Happiness is you
And all I need is Happiness

Questions

The questions you ask make us or break us
You can trust me blindly and believe in us
Or you can ask me endlessly and shatter
whatever is left of us
There's no us without trust
Not everything is questionable
The questions you ask
Should not be asked

Lights

Lights on, all of the lights
Collared shirt, buttoned up
Perfume fills the air, choking you
All the lights are on you
As you pat your cheeks with blush
As you draw the wing on your eyelid
As you pucker your lips and gloss with red
Your under the lights and all eyes are on you
Lights
Camera
Action

Red Roses

Roses
Bright, red, and full of life
But you can't have a rose without thorns
And the thorns bring pain
And then there behind the angel, with its wings
and halo, there's a devil, with its blaring horns
Crazy how the color red brings you the beauty of
roses, and the curse of the devil
And the beautiful roses
Erase the pain from its thorns

Rooftop nights

Nights on the rooftop
Lights are dimmed
Music is soaring
Smoke is flowing
Feel the light on your closed eyes
And the heat of the air around you
Nights like this are all you need
To forget the nights you wished never existed
Rooftop nights

Summer love

Temporary stay
Permanent feelings
You meet on the third day
Instantly finish healing
You walk around these people you don't know
With your head held up high
Noone has the right to know
How hard it was to get by
You love the summer
But you found love
It was supposed to be temporary
But the sign is from above
He's the one, your eyes say
You'll swear by from here on out
He's just a summer love, your lips
Yeah? Tell me what thats all about

Broken in peace

I wasn't whole when I met you
I was broken beyond repair
I fell in love with all of my pieces
I hoped you would just try to care
I didn't feel good about it
I didn't even try to hide it
As broken as I was feeling
I was beautiful in a way
To be broken, but in healing
Stitched together, but in peace

White dress

White dress, down to your toes
Sparkly shoes under the tail
Only family invited, no friends or foes
Makeup bringing out your every detail
The glow in your eyes
The brightness in your smile
Happiness needs no disguise
You've waited for the longest while
In a white dress, here you are
Queen of the day, shining like a star

Here's to us. Or what this could be.

Here we are at another ceremony Gathering
loved ones in holy matrimony
Seven years later we meet again
And as i guess youre with someone else
And I'm still thinking of way back when
Your feelings for me are on the back of the shelf
Or so I thought, until your eyes caught mine
Dinner is served, red or white wine?
Whichever you'll have I will too
You say
I take the stronger one, I need to get away
We sit down around everyone, away from one
another
You raise your glass, here's to my brother as you
smile at me
I click my glass against yours, here's to us, or
what this could be.